D0356902

THE
EXONERATED

BY JESSICA BLANK
AND ERIK JENSEN

★

★

DRAMATISTS
PLAY SERVICE
INC.

SPECIAL NOTE

SPECIAL NOTE ON POETRY

For the exonerated
and for those who are still waiting

INTRODUCTION

Over the summer of 2000, we traveled across the United States, sat in people's living rooms and listened as they told us what it was like to be wrongly convicted and on death row. They were from vastly different ethnic, religious and educational backgrounds. Their views on the world varied greatly. The only thing they held in common was that they had each been sentenced to die, spent anywhere from two to twenty-two years on death row, had subsequently had their convictions reversed and been freed by the state. We interviewed forty people on the phone and twenty in person. Six of these interviews form the core of *The Exonerated*.

That spring, we had gotten the idea for the play at a conference on the death penalty at Columbia University. We brought the idea to producer Allan Buchman, a friend of ours from the downtown theater community in New York.

Governor George Ryan of Illinois had just declared a moratorium on the death penalty in his state, and another George was running for high office — with more executions carried out under his watch as governor of Texas than in any other state since the reinstatement of the death penalty in 1976. The issue was very much in the news. Allan told us we could have his theater for three nights in the fall if we could have something up before the elections. So we hit the road. We went as far north and west as Chicago, as far south as Texas and Miami and just about everywhere in between to meet the people whose stories appear in this play.

We returned from the interviews with hours and hours of tape, which became several hundred pages of transcripts. We're both primarily actors, which means we have lots of talented and underemployed friends. We enlisted them to come workshop the transcripts with us and began the process of shaping hundreds of pages of everyday speech into a play. At the same time, we called director Bob Balaban and asked him to direct three readings of the play at Allan's theater that fall. Bob brought his highly trained eye to the material we were developing, as well as helping us assemble a cast for the readings that included Gabriel Byrne, Ossie Davis, Vincent D'Onofrio, Charles Dutton, Cherry Jones, David Morse, Susan Sarandon, Tim Robbins, Debra Winger and many other extraordinary actors. They performed an initial version of the play that consisted of the stories of twelve exonerated people, taken entirely from the interviews we had conducted.

After three readings at The Culture Project and a performance at the United Nations, we hit the road again. It was clear to us, Bob and our audiences how the exonerated people felt about what had happened to them; what was still unclear was how it could've happened in the first place. So we went through the extremely difficult process of paring down the number of stories in the play, in order to tell each one more fully. Additionally, we dug into the court transcripts and case files of the people whose stories we were telling. We spent countless hours in dusty courthouse record rooms, pawing through thousands of microfiche files and cardboard boxes full of affidavits, depositions, police interrogations and courtroom testimony. The court employees assumed we were law students — and we did nothing to discourage that belief. With a few exceptions, each word spoken in this play comes from the public record — legal documents, court transcripts, letters — or from an interview with an exonerated person. The names of the exonerated people are their own; some names of auxiliary characters have been changed for legal reasons.

The vast majority of the piece is as it was said two, five, ten and twenty years ago by the actual participants. At the time we conducted these interviews, there were 89 people who had been exonerated from death row. As of this writing there are now 102. We consider every one of their stories to be part of this play.

TO PRESENTERS INTERESTED
IN PRODUCING *THE EXONERATED*

Thank you for your interest in our play! As you proceed, you will find that this is a work that not only affects its audiences deeply, but also has the potential to change real people's lives for the better in a very immediate and material way.

As you may or may not know, there is no automatic restitution for the wrongfully convicted upon their release from prison; further, in most states, they are forbidden to sue. Further, it is enormously difficult to convince employers to hire someone just released from prison, even when that individual was imprisoned for a crime that evidence shows he or she didn't commit. There are virtually no resources in place to assist the wrongfully convicted in their transitions back into society; the vast majority reenter a world where it is nearly impossible for them to make a living.

From the play's inception, the writers, director and producers of *The Exonerated* have been dedicated to righting this wrong in the cases of the individuals whose stories appear in our play. Since the play first opened, we have raised a considerable amount of money for the real-life exonerated. They share in the profits from the production and receive a significant portion of all our incomes; but perhaps more importantly, they receive donations from individual audience members who have heard and been touched by their stories. After every performance of the play, a cast member steps forward to share the fact that the wrongfully convicted receive no automatic restitution for their many years lost, and invites audience members to give whatever they are moved to give on their way out of the theatre. These donations are collected by ushers and are immediately deposited into a nonprofit fund administered by the Culture Project (the play's original producer), which distributes all collected funds among the real-life exonerated.

The money raised through this simple process over the last few years has transformed the exonerateds' lives, while providing a way for audiences to make a real difference in a direct and satisfying way. The process has been an overwhelmingly positive and rewarding one for everyone involved: the theatres all across the country who have participated, the audience members, and most importantly, the exonerated people themselves, without whose courage and generosity in telling their stories none of this would be possible.

As the creators of *The Exonerated*, we feel that this collections process is an integral part of the play. It encapsulates and expresses the spirit in which the play was conceived and created. Provided your organization's rules allow for such collections, it is deeply important to us that you assist us in preserving that spirit as the play goes out into the world. There are real people behind the stories in *The Exonerated*, and you have an opportunity to help transform their lives profoundly, through a simple process that requires minimal effort on your part.

There are a variety of ways to request this kind of participation from audience members; we have found the post-show speech from the stage to be most effective and strongly suggest you use this method, but you can also prominently display a collections box in the lobby, enclose an insert in the program, etc. After your ushers collect the donations, please send them to *The Exonerated* Fund, c/o The Culture Project, 49 Bleecker St., 4th Floor, New York, NY 10012. (The Culture Project is a 401c3 organization; the Fund has been distributing contributions solely to the exonerated since the play opened in 2002.) As you do this, please know that you are using theatre to make a real and undeniable difference in people's lives and in the world.

NOTES ON THE PERFORMANCE OF THE PLAY

The first full production of *The Exonerated* was at the Actors' Gang in Los Angeles. Six months later, it opened Off-Broadway at the 45 Bleecker Theater. The Actors' Gang production was fully staged, with entrances, exits, a scrim and simple set pieces; Bob Balaban's Off-Broadway production was performed by ten actors seated in chairs for the duration of the play, with all environments and scene changes defined by lights and sound. Both ways of presenting the play worked, not least because both were minimal and unfussy, with the focus on the stories and on the actors who were telling them. This is a good rule of thumb for directors staging *The Exonerated*. It works either fully staged or with seated actors in a "story theater" format, as long as both the staging and storytelling are kept very simple.

Directors and actors should be careful not to be didactic in their presentation of the play. The drama of these stories does not need enhancement: It's generally a good idea to avoid stapling newspaper headlines to the back wall or throwing electric chairs all over the stage. Similarly, actors playing exonerated people should avoid overemotionalizing. These characters have been exonerated for a number of years. They have, of course, been deeply affected by their experiences in varying ways, all of which are integral to the play — but, except for a few instances, they are telling their stories, not reliving them. Trust the stories.

Also, all should keep in mind that because of the subject matter, things can get overly dark rather quickly. There are undeniably dramatic moments in the play — but remember that these are six stories of people who survived. There's a great deal of humor here, too — don't overlook it.

There are ten actors. Six play one exonerated person each; two play wives of the exonerated; and two Male Ensemble actors play the supporting cast of characters. Ensemble actors should establish a strong and clear personality for each character they play. They should also pay attention to the geographical location of each of the stories they appear in, keep the dialects specific, and be careful not to get generic Southern for everything; it's an easy trap to fall into here.

All the actors, with the possible exception of the actor playing David, should take care to find the humor in their characters. It's pretty difficult to make it through an experience this harrowing without the ability to laugh sometimes. Too much gravity and depression bring the play down; the actor playing Delbert should be especially careful about this. Delbert has an extraordinary sense of humor about himself and the world; to play only his gravitas is to do him a disservice.

Because the death penalty itself is inextricably connected to race, it is important that white people play white people and black people play black people. We strongly support non-traditional casting in general; but in the case of this play, it dilutes the reality of many of the issues involved.

Finally, we ask that any actors and directors working on this play respect the exonerated people's privacy by refraining from contacting them directly. Research is important, but these individuals' privacy and comfort are more so. Besides, in the process of watching over 100 actors work on these roles, we've found that actors usually do better when they don't meet the real people and/or watch videotape of them during the rehearsal process. Over and over, we've seen completely disparate actors, after spending some time with these words, unintentionally begin to channel the people they are play-ing, down to their speech patterns and mannerisms. It happens involuntarily and has nothing to do with mimicry or impersonation.

It's all in the words, and in the stories.

THE EXONERATED was originally presented in Los Angeles by the Actors' Gang (Tim Robbins, Artistic Director), in association with The Culture Project, on April 19, 2002. It was directed by Jessica Blank and Erik Jensen with supervision by Bob Balaban; the set design was by Richard Hoover; the original music and sound design were by David Robbins; the costume design was by Ann Closs-Farley; the managing director was Greg Reiner; and the production stage manager was Leah Harrison. The cast was as follows:

KERRY	Ken Palmer
SUNNY	Adele Robbins
SUE, SANDRA	Victoria Cunningham
DELBERT	Richard Lawson
ROBERT	Ken Elliott
MALE ENSEMBLE #1	Kelly Cole
MALE ENSEMBLE #2	Jon Kellam
MALE ENSEMBLE #3	Terrell Tilford
FEMALE ENSEMBLE	Blaire Chandler
DAVID	Ben Cain
GARY	Brian Powell
GEORGIA, JUDGE, DARLA, STATE PROSECUTOR	Yolanda Snowball

THE EXONERATED premiered in New York City at 45 Bleecker Theatre on October 10, 2002. It was produced by The Culture Project, Dede Harris, Morton Swinsky, Bob Balaban, Harit Allan Buchman, Patrick Blake, David Elliot, Jane Bergere, Ruth Hendel and Cheryl Wiesenfeld. It was directed by Bob Balaban; the set design was by Tom Ontiveros; the original music and sound design were by David Robbins; the costume design was by Sara J. Tosetti; and the production stage manager was Thomas J. Gates. The cast was as follows:

KERRY .... Richard Dreyfuss
SUNNY .... Jill Clayburgh
SUE, SANDRA .... Sara Gilbert
DELBERT .... Charles Brown
ROBERT .... David Brown Jr.
MALE ENSEMBLE #1 .... Bruce Kronenberg
MALE ENSEMBLE #2 .... Phil Levy
DAVID .... Curtis McClarin
GARY .... Jay O. Sanders
GEORGIA, JUDGE, DARLA,
STATE PROSECUTOR .... April Yvette Thompson

CHARACTERS

DELBERT, African-American, 60. A seminary dropout, radical and poet. His whole personality is like an old soul song: smooth, mellow and with an underlying rhythm that never lets up. Actors playing Delbert should take care to find his substantial sense of humor, in addition to his obvious depth.

SUNNY, white, 50. A bright, pixie-ish yoga teacher from California; her lightness and positivity contrast with moments of great depth and clarity.

ROBERT, African-American, 30s. A former horse groomer from the deep South; hardened but not lacking a sense of humor. Deep rural Mississippi accent.

GEORGIA/FEMALE ENSEMBLE 1, African-American, 30s. Robert's wife, also Southern; opinionated, outspoken and extremely warm. She and Robert have a lovingly contentious relationship. Loves to speak her mind.

GARY, white, 45. A Midwestern hippie and an organic farmer. Clearly was in his element in the late 60s and early 70s. He is generally good-natured, friendly and quite smart.

KERRY, white, 45. A 19-year-old trapped in a 45-year-old's body, born and bred in Texas. Kerry was imprisoned for 22 of his 45 years and is eager to rediscover the world. Always wants to make sure he connects with whomever he is talking to. Strong Texas accent.

DAVID, African-American, 40. A gentle, sad man, born and raised in northern Florida (otherwise known as southern Alabama). Has a very strong spiritual sense and had aspirations to the ministry before being put on death row at 18. He is continually engaged in a battle between resignation and hope.

SANDRA/SUE/FEMALE ENSEMBLE 2, white, 40. Sandra is married to Kerry. Sweet, nurturing, loves Kerry dearly and has a great sense of humor about him. She has a strong Texas accent. Sue is married to Gary. Salt of the earth; she is also an organic farmer. She has a *strong* upper Midwestern accent — think *Fargo*.

MALE ENSEMBLE 1 and 2, both white, 35–50. Male Ensemble 1 and 2 play police officers, attorneys, suspects and other supporting characters. Both actors should be good with dialects and characterization, and different from each other in build and appearance. Both roles require highly versatile, commanding actors. Character assignments for ensemble actors appear on the following page.

MALE ENSEMBLE 1 plays WHITE COP 1, KERRY'S DEFENSE, SHERIFF CARROLL, JESSE, COURT ATTORNEY, DAVID'S PROSECUTOR, VOICEOVER/INMATE, WHITE GUARD, JEFF, CELLMATE, EX-BOYFRIEND and FARMER.

MALE ENSEMBLE 2 plays WHITE COP 2, KERRY'S PROSECUTION, RHODES, DEPUTY, SOUTHERN WHITE GUY, ROBERT'S JUDGE, DAVID'S DEFENSE, DOYLE and THE PROSECUTION.

FEMALE ENSEMBLE 1 (GEORGIA) also plays STATE ATTORNEY, KERRY'S JUDGE and DARLA.

FEMALE ENSEMBLE 2 (SANDRA/SUE) also plays FEMALE LAWYER.

The roles of BLACK COP, BLACK GUY 1 and BLACK INMATE are played by the actor who plays DAVID.

The role of BLACK GUY 2 is played by the actor who plays ROBERT.

SETTING

Bare stage; minimal set with several chairs and multiple entrances and exits. Can be performed in proscenium, in the round, or by seated actors.

THE EXONERATED

Open on a stage, bare except for ten plain, armless chairs. These chairs can be used variously to set up scenes throughout the piece. The entire play can be performed using only these chairs. No further set pieces are necessary, although tables and other set pieces might work too. The play is seamless: There are no blackouts during the performance and no intermission. Unless otherwise noted, the exonerated people deliver their monologues to the audience. Delbert can see the other exonerated people; unless otherwise noted, none of the other exonerated people see each other or Delbert. At various points in the play we see "scenes" illustrating the stories being told by the exonerated. These scenes exist in the exonerated people's memories, and unless otherwise noted, should take place behind or beside the character telling the story.

Delbert functions as a sort of Chorus, fading in and out of the action. He is a black man in his late fifties. His whole personality is like an old soul song: smooth, mellow, but with a relentless underlying rhythm. He has a great sense of humor. He's from Chicago.

DELBERT.
This is not the place for thought that does not end in concreteness;
it is not easy to be open or too curious.
It is dangerous to dwell too much on things:
to wonder who or why or when, to wonder how, is dangerous.
How do we, the people, get outta this hole, what's the way to fight,
might I do what Richard and Ralph and Langston'n them did?
It is not easy to be a poet here. Yet I sing.
I sing.

(Lights up on Sue and Gary. Sue is Gary's wife. Farmer woman, salt of the earth. She has a very strong upper Midwest accent — think Fargo. Gary is a Midwestern hippie in his mid-forties. He is an organic farmer. He was clearly in his element in the late sixties and early seventies. He is generally good-natured and quite smart.)

GARY. Gary Gauger. This is my wife, Sue. *(Beat; Sue waves.)* So my case — the day before, I had gone to work here, you see our workshop is a little building right over there. And it is about ninety-two percent recycled.

SUE. Even the shingles and the foundation are recycled.

GARY. So anyway, I start my plants out there, and then in mid-March we move 'em out front to the hotbeds. So I would come over here in the morning and work all day, and I'd go back for supper at night.

So anyways, that day, I went to work, my folks weren't around —

SUE. But they had been planning a trip to Sugar Grove —

GARY. I just thought, "No big deal, they go away sometimes." By night, they didn't get home, I was worried about 'em. I said, "Jeez, they must've gotten in a car accident." But what do you do, call hospitals?

SUE. Oh, ya can't. Ya can't. Not between here and Sugar Grove.

GARY. And the police, I knew, wouldn't investigate until they'd been missing for twenty-four hours. So I just basically stayed by the phone till midnight, went to bed.

Next morning, I got up to call the police, and a customer came walkin' up the driveway, looking for motorcycle parts, and in the back room where we thought the part might be is where we found my father's body.

Now, it looked to me like he'd suffered a stroke, because he was face down in a pool of blood. And he obviously … was dead. I felt his pulse.

So, all of a sudden, here's my father's body, my mom's been missing. So I called the paramedics, who called the police, who told me they suspect foul play.

About an hour and a half later, they find my mother's body in a trailer out in front of the house. She had been killed and covered with rugs and pillows. *(Pause.)* They had been hidden, and their throats were slashed.

Two and a half hours after I found my parents, they had me arrested. *(Lights down on Gary and Sue, up on Delbert.)*

16

DELBERT.
    It is not easy:
    you stand waiting for a train
    or a bus that may never come
    no friend drives by to catch a ride
    cold, tired:
    call yourself a poet
    but work all day mopping floors and looking out for thieves ...
(Lights down on Delbert, up on Robert and his wife Georgia. Robert is a black man in his mid-thirties, hardened but not lacking a sense of humor, with a deep rural Mississippi accent. Georgia is also Southern; opinionated, earthy, contentious and extremely warm. Loves to speak her mind. The two of them overlap, finish each other's sentences, and otherwise play off each other whenever they appear together.)

ROBERT. Robert Earl Hayes. This here's my wife —

GEORGIA. Georgia Hayes.

ROBERT. *(Sotto voce.)* Baby, they know your last name —

GEORGIA. I know, I just wanted to introduce myself. Go ahead.

ROBERT. Now, at the time that all this happened I was working around the racetrack, takin' care of the horses you know. And at that racetrack, this white girl, she gets raped and killed. And you know, she be dating the black guys —

GEORGIA. Mm-hmm.

ROBERT. — and when she got killed, they ask me have I ever had sex with the girl. I told them yeah, they said —

WHITE COP 1. Well, were you having sex with her that night?

ROBERT. I said no. Then they said —

WHITE COP 1. Well, why does she like hanging out on the black side of the track?

ROBERT. So I said, "I don't know why she like hanging out back there, I guess we more fun."
    But this girl, she got killed. And the cop came to my job the next morning, they said —

WHITE COP 1. We gotta talk to you.

ROBERT. I said okay, I went to the police station. And they kept saying —

WHITE COP 2. We know what happened —

WHITE COP 1. We know you asked her for a date, and she hit you —

WHITE COP 2. — and you hit her back —

WHITE COP 1. — and you didn't *mean* to hit her that hard. *(Lights down on cops.)*

ROBERT. They just came right after me. This white girl, me and she had dated, and you know people 'round here don't like that too much.

GEORGIA. Mm-hmm.

ROBERT. And in my first trial I *knew* I was going to prison — I had eleven whites and one black on that jury.

GEORGIA. And do you think, seriously, now be honest, if the roles had been reversed, if it had been a black woman and a white man, it woulda been like that?

ROBERT. Right, 'cause let's go to another high-profile case.

GEORGIA. Oh, here we go —

ROBERT. Now within all y'all's hearts — now be honest — within your *heart*, do you really think O.J. committed that crime?

GEORGIA. *(Laughing.)* Well, but O.J., you know, I'm black and I *still* think he guilty, I'm sorry — I don't care what they say, if the DNA put you there, O.J., you guilty. *(Lights down on Robert and Georgia, up on Kerry and Sandra. Kerry is an eager nineteen-year-old trapped in a forty-five-year-old's body, white, with a Texas accent. Kerry is an "up-talker" — he ends many of his sentences with a question mark. Sandra is Kerry's wife, also Texan, very pregnant, very sweet, takes care of Kerry.)*

KERRY. Kerry Max Cook. *(Beat.)*

SANDRA. Sandra Cook.

KERRY. It actually started when I was in the ninth or tenth grade: Me and my friends would, you know, act like we were going to school and then run out the back door and start trying to find a car with the keys in it. And I had the misfortune that one of the cars that I stole, in my adventures to conquer the world, was the sheriff deputy's car and I, ah … wrecked it — driver's ed I didn't take — and, make a long story short, the deputy beat me for it.

And that was pretty much it — after that, any robbery, any broken window, any cat up a tree, everything was just *my fault,* as far as the sheriff was concerned.

And then fast forwarding, I'm nineteen, and I'm at this apartment complex in Texas called the Embarcadero — there's a swimming pool there, it's where all the hip people hang out. And I was an attractive guy, I dressed real nice. It was the seventies you know, man: I bought my clothes from the hippest place, like the Gap, and

18

I had my hair styled real long, platform shoes and bell-bottoms. I looked tight. And I was walkin' towards the swimming pool, and there was this beautiful gorgeous girl, man. *(To Sandra.)* Not as pretty as you.

SANDRA. Go on.

KERRY. But really *gorgeous*, man — just nude and fondling herself, right there in the window. So I look up and I go, "Oh my god, man … wow," cause I had lived a very sheltered, naïve life, I'd never even been to a strip club before, and I'm seeing this total complete mature woman, and I'm goin' "okay, yeah, that's cool, man."

And so anyway, a couple days go by, and I'm back at the pool and there's this chick, layin' out there. To make a long story short, we started talking, told her I was a bartender in Dallas — 'course I was working at a gay bar, but I didn't tell her that — I'm just stretching everything as much as I can because I want to be all that plus a bag of potater chips. Anyway, we end up going back to her apartment … we … uh … you know … made out.

SANDRA. *(To audience.)* But not — all the way.

KERRY. Oh, no, no, no. I was in there for about maybe thirty, forty-five minutes, whatever, and I got cold feet because she was so aggressive, and I left.

And I didn't ever see or hear from her ever again until I'm arrested for her murder three months later, August of 1977. *(Sound of gavel. Lights up on Kerry's defense, prosecution and judge. They speak facing the audience.)*

KERRY'S DEFENSE. Since June 10, 1977, Tyler, Texas, has been screaming and crying for *someone* to answer this crime —

KERRY'S PROSECUTION. *(Thick Texas accent.)* The state of Texas would object to that being far beyond the scope of this case —

KERRY'S JUDGE. I am going to sustain that objection. *(Courtroom freezes.)*

KERRY. They had found a fingerprint of mine on her doorframe.

SANDRA. And they had a fingerprint guy whose knowledge of fingerprints at that point was a six-month correspondence school — *(Courtroom back in action.)*

PROSECUTION. *(Overlapping.)* Lieutenant Doug Collins is an expert fingerprint technologist. He will testify that he found a fingerprint belonging to the defendant, Kerry Max Cook. It is as clear, Ladies and Gentlemen, as the day when you put your footprint on your birth certificate. That officer didn't have any reason to lie. He will narrow the time element of the leaving of those fingerprints —

DEFENSE. Objection, your Honor.

KERRY. *(To audience.)* You *can't* date a fingerprint, it's scientifically impossible.

DEFENSE. It cannot be proven what time those prints were made. This would place in the minds of the jurors that the defendant was there at the time of the murder!

JUDGE. Is that all you have?

DEFENSE. Yes, ma'am.

JUDGE. Your motion is overruled.

KERRY. That judge let them say, all through my trial, that I left that fingerprint there at the time of her murder.

And this next part has all been hidden for twenty years: Linda, the victim, had been having an affair with this guy Whitfield, a professor of sciences over at the University, and *everyone* had just found out about it, he was fired from his job, lost his wife, lost his kids, whole big mess. And her roommate, Darla, had seen somebody in the apartment the night of the murder, who she said had silver hair, medium-short, touching-the-ears fashion, wearing white tennis shorts. Just like Whitfield.

In her police report, Darla says she sees this guy Whitfield in the apartment that night and says — *(Lights up on Darla.)*

DARLA. Don't worry, it's only me.

KERRY. — and goes to bed. But at the trial she turns around and says —

DARLA. *(Pointing.)* That's the man right there.

KERRY. — and points at me. *(Lights down on Darla and courtroom.)* And my lawyer didn't even argue with that. My attorney was the former D.A. who jailed me twice before. He was paid 500 dollars, and in Texas, you get what you pay for. *(Lights down on Kerry and Sandra; up on Delbert.)*

DELBERT.
It's not easy to find some quiet place.
Some grace. No time
to talk about dreams
in this world
where ice
is everywhere.

(Lights down on Delbert; up on David.)

DAVID. David Keaton.

At the time they pulled me in, I was in high school. I had a lotta thoughts of what I was gonna do, where I was gonna go, where I

20

should be, ten years from there, you know. I was, as some might say, I was called to the ministry.

But I mean the way they picked me up — me and some friends was comin' from a movie that day and we saw a big commotion, and we said, "man, what's goin' on?" So we run down, and the cops are all round here, shinin' their lights up on my grandmother's house.

And we was just standin' there watchin', and the cop says — *(Lights up on deputy.)*

DEPUTY. Do any of y'all know David Keaton?

DAVID. And boy, here I am like a nut, "I am he."

So they took me down to the station and interrogated me, askin' me about this robbery, and I just kept sayin' to them over and over, "I don't know what you're talkin' about. I don't know what you're talkin' about. I don't know what you're talkin' about." But they locked the doors, they held me incommunicado, as you might say.

When they first brought me into the jail, one of the deputies asked the sheriff at that time — *(Lights up on Carroll.)*

DEPUTY. *(Southern accent.)* You gonna keep him?

DAVID. And the sheriff said —

SHERIFF CARROLL. *(Thick Southern accent.)* You're goddamn right, we gonna keep him.

DAVID. The sheriff was running for re-election at the time, and this was a big unsolved crime, so he had to bring somebody in for it. And they're tellin' me what happened in the crime, who was standin' where and all of that, and I mean I don't even know what the store looks like, and they're yellin' at me, tryin to get me to describe it. *(Lights dim slightly on David throughout the following.)*

DEPUTY. This interview is being given with Deputy Sheriff H.M. Carroll. Mr. Carroll, if you will, explain to me the events that took place at Luke's Grocery on September 18th, 1970, as they relate to the case of David Keaton.

CARROLL. Well, about two-thirty Officer Khomas Revels and myself went in, I went over to the tobacco counter to get some chaw and he walked on back toward the milk case. And then I heard a nigger tell him, "get on over there, I ain't got no time to fool with you," so I walked on around to where Khomas was at. And this boy, he had a gun, just said, "don't give us no trouble." And he had ah, kind of an Afro haircut, not a full Afro, but he looked like he was tryin' to grow him some Afro hair. And he had a little mustache, best I can remember, I mean everything was goin' so fast there. And the other one that was standin' over where they

21

had about five or six customers tied down, he was around six foot tall. And the third sonofabitch — on his forehead, looked like he had, I don't know, you've seen them with kind of a scar sometimes?

DEPUTY. Oh yeah.

CARROLL. Anyway, they told us to give them our money. So we did, 'bout thirty-two dollars, and then they said we want them watches too. Well, we didn't either one of us pull our watches off.

And they told us to lay down. So we did, and one of them, he reached over to get him some panty hose to tie us up with — but myself and Khomas, we came up and tackled them. Ain't nobody gonna be tyin' me up with no panty hose. And so the other one, he come running down shooting at us.

They must have shot eighteen or twenty bullets during the ruckus there, and the two hit me, and the two hit Khomas. And I could see that he was dead. *(Extended beat.)* And the niggers, they just disappeared.

DEPUTY. Mr. Carroll, in listening to these people talk in the store, did they have any type of accent, did they sound like local people or were they from out of state?

CARROLL. Naw, they just sounded like regular niggers to me. *(Lights down on deputy and Carroll; full up on David.)*

DAVID. And I was just eighteen, I didn't know the rules. And they kept on talkin', and they were threatenin' me, and all that. And I was afraid. I mean they would go in there and beat you up, mess you up, hang you up, nobody'd ever hear nothin' else about you. And so I say, okay, to prevent that, I'm gonna go ahead and confess to the crime. I know I'm tellin' the truth, and the witnesses are gonna know too, 'cause I just wasn't there and they would have seen that. So I'm like, I'm gonna let them go ahead, they gave me all the information already, all I do is put some names to the spots and then we all can be free. *(Lights down on David; up on Sunny.)*

SUNNY. Sunny Jacobs. *(Beat.)* In 1976, I was sentenced to death row, which for me wasn't a row at all because I was the only woman in the country who had the sentence of death. So *I* suggested they put me in the same cell as my husband!

But let me start at the beginning. *(Beat.)*

When I was twenty-six, Jesse and I had been together for three years. We weren't officially married, but I considered him my husband, you know. Our daughter had just been born, and Jesse said he was gonna get himself a regular job, maybe painting murals or something, but he just needed to go to Florida one last time to do a little deal.

Now, I didn't want to know about this deal, because I knew it wasn't positive; it wasn't violent, but it wasn't positive. And finally he calls and says that the deal fell through, and not only is he broke and has no way home, but he's staying with some *girl!* So, of course, me, instead of saying, "well, when you get it together, me and the kids will be here waiting for you," I said, "I'll be right there to getcha!"

My son Eric was nine, and I was driving, shifting, singing and nursing Tina all at the same time. It was like driving through the ten plagues, you know, the first being the oil leaking all over the road, and the final one — you know those love bugs that smash themselves on your window?

So anyway, we get there, get Jesse, the car dies, and we're all stuck in Florida. And so Jesse says he'll ask this guy he knows if we can stay with him until we can scrape the money together to get home.

And that's when I met Walter Rhodes.

So we're all stuck in Florida, staying at Walter Rhodes' apartment. And it was a real sleazebag place; I mean he was obviously doing illegal activities. *(Lights up on Jesse and Rhodes.)*

JESSE. Hey Rhodes, we're gonna take off. Could you give us a lift to my friend's over in Broward County?

RHODES. I don't know, man, it's late — I don't know if I want to be on the road —

JESSE. Come on man, nothing ever happens in Broward. *(Lights down on Jesse and Rhodes.)*

SUNNY. And it was so weird — my son Eric woke up screaming in the middle of the night. He had this nightmare that something terrible was going to happen to us. And it did. *(Lights down on Sunny, up on Delbert.)*

DELBERT.

It's not easy
to feel good in winter winds
when ice is everywhere
and you just wanna sing …

Copyright 1997, Delbert Tibbs … I'm Delbert Tibbs.

I'm a child of the sixties and the seventies, right? So, much of the philosophy that people were motivated by during those times I was, and continue to be, motivated by. I have an ongoing — an *abiding* interest in things philosophical and/or metaphysical; I won't say religious …

And so, you know, in 1972, I went to seminary for a year and a half, but the racism there was so pervasive you could cut it with a knife. So I decided that the seminary wasn't gonna take me where I wanted to go, so I dropped out, and started roaming America. We called it *tunin' in.* Tune in, turn on, an' drop out. And I haven't turned off for a long time.

So that's where I was at — and I happened to be in Florida when some crazy stuff happened, a guy was killed, a young woman was raped, and I happened to be in Florida.

And I knew that some folks were gonna say — *(Lights up on Southern White Guy.)*

SOUTHERN WHITE GUY. Now what's this nigga doin here, and who is he, an' why is he here?! *(Lights down on Southern White Guy.)*

DELBERT. — and so forth, but my attitude was fuck that, you know? I'm an American citizen, and I've served in the Armed Forces of the United States, and all that kinda shit.

The point I'm trying to make is that, in my mind I decided that I was gonna be free in terms a my movements. That I was gonna go wherever I wanted to go, in these United States, an' whatever came out of that, if there was trouble, then I would deal with it when it came. And sure enough … *(Chuckle.)* sure enough, trouble came.

(Beat.) Because this *crime* had occurred, and I was on the highway in Florida, so I was stopped and questioned, and the captain wrote me out a note sayin' — *(Lights up on White Cop 1.)*

WHITE COP 1. *(Unnaturally fast robotic monotone.)* This person was stopped by me on this date and I'm satisfied that he's not the person wanted in connection with the crimes that occurred in southern Florida. *(Lights down on White Cop 1.)*

DELBERT. Now, initially, the girl who survived the thing described the murderer as a black man about five six, very dark complexion, with pockmarked skin and a bush Afro. *(Beat.)* Now that don't fit me no matter how you draw it — except racially. That's the only thing we had in common: We're both black men.

But now it's like two weeks or something after the crime has occurred, and they gotta find *somebody,* cause the small town is in hysterics, you know? There's a nigger running around killing white men and raping white women, and you can't have that. *(Beat.)* Understandably.

So anyway, the cops stopped me again, and I said no, I'm not. I said I was stopped in Florida — *(Lights up on White Cop 1.)*

WHITE COP 1. *(Again, unnaturally fast robotic monotone.)* This person was stopped by me on this date and — *(Lights down on*

White Cop 1.)
DELBERT. *(Interrupting.)* — and to the satisfaction of the Florida Highway Patrol, I'm not the person that you're looking for. He says, in effect:
WHITE COP 2. Bullshit.
DELBERT. He says —
WHITE COP 2. You're Delbert Tibbs, I have a warrant for your arrest.
DELBERT. And they arrested me in Mississippi. *(Lights down on Delbert and White Cop 2, up on Robert and Georgia.)*
ROBERT. *(To Georgia.)* — I mean, I might as well be wearin' a sign that says, "arrest me, I'm black."
GEORGIA. *(To Audience.)* It's always somethin'. I mean it's not all police officers, it's not all white people, but it's those few that make the rest of them look so bad —
ROBERT. *(To Audience.)* But I mean, hypothetically speaking, if me and a white woman have an altercation, the cop gonna say well, it's OK for her. But for me, all she got to say is, "He touched my breast. He touched my booty," and there go the wildfire.
GEORGIA. It's not only just whites; it's blacks too —
ROBERT. *(Interrupting.)* Not to cut you off, but one night, me and a white guy, we were sitting at a gas station. We were just sitting there talking, and a white cop came back around to talk to us. *(Lights up on White Cop 1 and Southern White Guy.)*
ROBERT. And he didn't ask me was I having a problem, he asked the white guy was *he* having a problem. He says —
WHITE COP 1. I see both you guys talking and moving your hands.
ROBERT. — and you know, the black person talk with his hands, if you guys haven't noticed. The white guy, he said —
SOUTHERN WHITE GUY. No, me and Robert just sitting up here talking.
ROBERT. And the cop said —
WHITE COP 1. Do you know Robert?
SOUTHERN WHITE GUY. Yeah, I been knowing him for the longest.
ROBERT. But the cop said —
WHITE COP 1. Oh, I thought he was harassing you.
GEORGIA. Okay?! *(Lights down on Cop and Southern White Guy.)*
ROBERT. I mean, God put everyone on earth, God put the ass, he put the fleas, but there's a lot of white people that make me

upset. But I'm not gonna call them crackers and go and get my cousin and all that.

GEORGIA. *(Sotto voce, overlapping.)* No, don't get your cousin; your cousin *crazy.*

ROBERT. I think if anyone have anything against anyone in this country, it should have been the Indians. But I do think now, these days, it's a lot better, especially in Mississippi because if it wasn't, I'd be sittin' here saying, "yes ma'am, Miss Daisy." Maybe it's goin' away —

GEORGIA. *(Interrupting.)* But Robert — *(To Audience.)* Okay, in my opinion, you never gonna get rid of it. My father taught me, things are passed down from generation to generation, and if the older generation teach the younger generation, then it ain't never gonna go away. *(Lights down on Robert and Georgia; up on Delbert.)*

DELBERT.

No time in this world to talk about dreams,
no space to place words in some lovely configuration;
deliberation is not the method
for passage through these woods
cold, tired
if you dream in this world
it is dangerous

(Lights down on Delbert, up on Sunny.)

SUNNY. My son Eric couldn't sleep because of the nightmare, and I just couldn't stay with Rhodes another night. So finally Rhodes agreed to give me, Jesse and the kids a ride.

And we left, but the traffic got bad and it was getting late, so the decision was made to pull off the road until morning. *(Dim light up on Black Cop, Jesse, Rhodes.)* And according to the police reports, the cops came to do a routine check on the rest area. And when they look in the window, they see a gun between Rhodes' feet. They order him out of the car and ask for his ID. The policeman calls in the ID information, and then tells Rhodes:

BLACK COP. Stand over there, I'm finished with you.

SUNNY. And then they ask my husband Jesse to get out.

And then the police radio comes back with the announcement that Rhodes is on parole — and possession of a gun is a parole violation.

And that changed everything. The policeman drew his gun. He said —

BLACK COP. Okay, the next one to move is dead.

26

SUNNY. It all happened so fast, you know. I just ducked down to cover the kids. *(Four loud gunshots.)* And then it was silence. I mean *dead silence*. There wasn't an earthly sound.

And then Rhodes runs around the front of the police car with a gun in his hand, and he's saying —

RHODES. Come on, we're gonna take the police car!

SUNNY. I mean, Rhodes had just killed two policemen, had a gun and was telling us to get in the police car. And, you know, people say, "Why didn't you just refuse to go?" And I think, you've never been at the other end of a gun, have you?

So we get in the police car. We couldn't speak. *(Cars honking/helicopters.)* We were kidnapped at that point, and we just didn't dare.

But then all of a sudden, the traffic gets terrible, and you can hear the helicopters, and I know there must be a roadblock. "Hey, we're gonna be *rescued!* Help is on the way, you know, the cavalry!"

And out of nowhere Rhodes makes a sharp left to try and avoid the roadblock — *(Heavy gunfire.)* — and this whole line of policemen opens fire on the car. The car was literally bouncing with all the bullets. So again I cover the kids. And finally we crash. *(Crash/sirens.)* And a bunch of cops surround us, and I'm trying to explain that we were kidnapped, but they just wouldn't listen. *(Lights shift; we are now in Sunny's interrogation room.)*

WHITE COP 1. All right. Sonia, or do you want me to call you Sunny?

SUNNY. It doesn't matter.

WHITE COP 2. *(Interrupting, to Sunny.)* Do you know what the date today is?

SUNNY. I think it's the twentieth.

WHITE COP 2. Is it Friday?

WHITE COP 1. *(Jumping in.)* Let me inject one thing here. Are you aware of the fact that you have been charged and arrested on First Degree Murder?

SUNNY. *(Beat.)* You just told me now. *(Lights down on Sunny and Cops, up on Gary.)*

GARY. I took a polygraph test around midnight. They wouldn't let me sleep, wouldn't let me lie down — and the polygraph examiner said he cannot pass me because of flat lines due to *fatigue*. Well, *duh*, it's midnight, I'd been under questioning now for six hours, and my parents had just been *murdered*.

About one A.M., they got three or four photos of my parents with their heads pulled back, you could look down their throat,

and the detective's yelling — *(Lights up on Cops.)*
WHITE COP 1. How could you do this?
WHITE COP 2. *(Overlapping.)* How could you kill this woman?
WHITE COP 1. *(Overlapping.)* The person who gave birth to you!
(Lights down on Cops.)
GARY. And this is how the interrogation went. I was in such a vulnerable and suggestible state from finding my parents and not knowing what happened. I was emotionally distraught, I was physically exhausted. I was confused. I had fifteen cups of coffee. I was spaced out. And the police used that. They said they had all the evidence, they didn't even *need* my confession. They said they had bloody fingerprints, the weapon, everything.

I was brainwashed, man. They told me —
WHITE COP 1 and WHITE COP 2. *(In unison, very friendly.)* We can't lie to you, or we'd lose our jobs.
GARY. They seemed very sincere, too. Very believable. They started making me think I had a blackout and actually done it. I said, look, if I killed my parents I want to know about it.

So I said, okay, if I could construct the situation in my mind — *(Small beat.)* I finally volunteered to give what they call a "vision statement" — a hypothetical account of what I would have done if I had killed my parents —
COPS. To try and jog your memory.
GARY. — to try and jog my memory. *(Lights down on White Cop 2. Gary begins "vision statement," trying to put it all together.)* Well, I guess I would've gotten up that morning —
WHITE COP 1. *(Testifying on the stand. Sure of what he's saying. His lines overlap tightly with Gary's — in the following section, the actors should speak over the ends of each other's lines.)* The defendant stated that he got up that morning —
GARY. And my mom would've been out in the trailer —
WHITE COP 1. — and that he looked outside and saw his mother in the trailer.
GARY. Then I woulda gotten dressed — and I would've had to have a knife in my pocket or something —
WHITE COP 1. And he indicated he put his pants on, and he had a knife in his pants pocket.
GARY. I guess I would've gone over to the trailer she was in —
WHITE COP 1. Then he walked up to the trailer and stepped onto the porch.
GARY. — and walked in —

28

WHITE COP 1. He said he opened the door, he walked in.

GARY. I would've had to have reached out toward my mom —

WHITE COP 1. He reached up and he grabbed his mother with his left hand and cut her throat with his right. *(Lights down on White Cop 1.)*

GARY. *(Beat.)* I never would've hurt her. *(Lights shift.)* They used that vision statement for a *confession.*

And they wouldn't let me say anything besides how I would've done it. Any time I tried to say anything else, they would just holler at me, and holler at me, and holler at me.

After I made the statement about my mom, I cried for about three minutes, and then I told them how I would have killed my father. And then I said, I *told* them, this is just hypothetical. I have absolutely no memory of any of this.

The autopsies showed that everything I said in those statements was wrong. But nothing was written down, nothing was recorded. At the trial, they said that I was never under arrest, I was free to go at any time, that I had voluntarily "chatted" with them for *twelve hours*, and then suddenly blurted out facts that only the killer would know. *(Lights down on Gary, up on Delbert.)*

DELBERT. Well, yeah, man, it definitely has an effect on you for people to lock you up: First of all, it shows you they have the power to do it, and then they tell you they're gonna kill you, you know, and you're inclined to believe them. *(Chuckles.)* So it definitely messes with your sense of personal power, you know what I'm saying? *(Lights up on Sunny, down on Delbert.)*

SUNNY. *(To audience.)* So I actually did at first try to lie, and I told the cops I didn't know these people, I was just a hitchhiker. Stupid. Because of course they think you're lying because you did something. But I was just scared. *(Lights shift; we are back in Sunny's interrogation room. Both cops keep the pressure intensely, relentlessly high on Sunny throughout the following.)*

WHITE COP 2. Let me ask you point blankly. Who shot the highway patrolman and the other officer?

SUNNY. I don't know.

WHITE COP 1. Did you shoot the highway patrolman?

SUNNY. No!

WHITE COP 2. Sunny, did you shoot anyone?

SUNNY. No.

WHITE COP 1. *(Yelling.)* DO YOU KNOW IF SOMEONE WAS SHOT?!

SUNNY. I'm *sorry*. People were shot. The patrolmen were shot and that's what this is all about — I don't know —

WHITE COP 2. *(Jumping down Sunny's throat.)* Well, how do you know that the two policemen are dead?

SUNNY. You said. That's what we're here for!

WHITE COP 2. Okay. We advised you that they were dead because we had — *(Continues to talk over Sunny's next line.)*

SUNNY. I didn't see. I didn't see —

WHITE COP 2. *(Talking over her.)* — we had to read you your rights and it's imperative that you relate the facts of this to the best of your ability. Something caused you to be very disturbed. What was that something?

SUNNY. *(Breaking down.)* This is very upsetting because how does — this guy, he told — he just told us to sit in the car, you know — and I'll stay here and I won't make any calls and I — I haven't done anything except the wrong choice of people and I —

WHITE COP 1. *(Very close to Sunny.)* But you do want to cooperate with the state of Florida?

SUNNY. Yeah, I —

WHITE COP 2. You're not *being* too cooperative because you're saying a lot of things you don't even remember and yet you were there. You were there, Sunny.

SUNNY. I'm sorry, I — I know but I never had anything like this happen to me before. I just — I don't want to be blamed for something that I had nothing to do with and I don't want them to take the kids away and I — cause the baby's crying and crying and crying and Eric's scared and I — I do want to help. I —

WHITE COP 1. All right, Sunny, I want you to help us.

SUNNY. Because I don't — I don't know what this guy was up to and I don't want to be pulled into it, but do you understand I'm trying to cooperate with —

WHITE COP 1. *(Condescending to her.)* Yes, sweetheart, I fully understand this.

SUNNY. And if I can't tell you everything you need to know please don't be angry with me.

WHITE COP 2. Okay, okay. *(Beat.)* Is there anything you care to add to your statement at this time?

SUNNY. I can't think of anything but if I do I will.

WHITE COP 1. *(An accusation.)* All right, are the answers you've given true and accurate to the best of your knowledge? *(Beat, as Sunny considers whether to tell the truth. Then, yelling:)* ANSWER ME!

SUNNY. *(Lying.)* Yes. *(Lights down on Cops; we are out of Sunny's interrogation room.)* And what I didn't know, was at the same moment I was being questioned and Jesse was being questioned, was that Rhodes, from his hospital bed, was negotiating a deal. He'd been in prison before, he knew how the system worked. And so he was claiming that he didn't do it — we did. *(Lights down on Sunny; up on State Attorney and Rhodes.)*

STATE ATTORNEY. Okay, Mr. Rhodes. Who had the gun in their hands when the first shot was fired?

RHODES. *(Overly helpful.)* When the gun first went off, Sonia was the one holding the gun. *(Then, scrambling:)* This is to the best of my knowledge, I am not one-hundred percent sure. To the best of my knowledge, she fired two shots, I believe then Jesse pulled the gun from her and shot him one more time and then he shot the other cop twice.

STATE ATTORNEY. Let me recap this now. To the best of your recollection, Sonia fired?

RHODES. First.

STATE ATTORNEY. It is your testimony here that Sonia fired the first three shots at the Florida Highway Patrolman?

RHODES. Either the first two or three.

STATE ATTORNEY. Two, or three?

RHODES. Two for sure.

STATE ATTORNEY. And then what took place?

RHODES. Then I started to go toward my car, to get in, it didn't even enter into my mind, but Jesse said get in the police car, we have got to get out of here or something and I said, "no," you know, "what happened?!" Anyway I did get in the police car, I was damn near in shock myself.

STATE ATTORNEY. Thank you.

RHODES. No problem. *(Lights down on Rhodes and Attorney, up on Delbert.)*

DELBERT. So I'm sitting there in Mississippi. After a couple days of being locked up, I decided I would waive extradition. Now this was because of my spiritual growth. A friend of mine has something he calls his "nigger radar," right, which sort of alerts him when, as he quotes Darth Vader, when there's a "disturbance in the force."

But I'm operating on another thing, you know, 'cause a lotta the *tension* I had felt regarding race had sorta been washed away. I had achieved some sort of spiritual ... plateau, if you will, by living out on the road.

31

I wasn't expecting any problems. I had been befriended by all kinda people — mostly white folks, 'cause there weren't no black folks around. I hitchhiked across Texas, which is as big as Russia, you know what I'm sayin'? And I got *one* ride from a brother. Brother picked me up, he said — *(Lights up on Black Guy.)*

BLACK GUY 1. Man, you know brothers don't hitchhike out here too much.

DELBERT. I know, but I don't have any money, what am I gonna do. *(Lights down on Black Guy.)* Anyway, I waived extradition to Florida, meaning I voluntarily went back. If I hadn't done that, I don't think I would've ever gone to death row, 'cause the state of Florida really didn't have a case. Nobody had seen me there, there was no connection between me and the place where the crime occurred, fingerprints, none'a that — 'cause I wasn't there.

And in Florida, as in most places, the jury is chosen from the voting records — and this is 1974, black people had only had the right to vote since 1965, and this is a backwater town where it's run sorta like a plantation and the folks in charge are the folks in charge, right?

And as I sometimes tell people, if you're accused of a sex crime in the South and you're black — you probably shoulda done it, you know, 'cause your ass is gonna be guilty. And they found me guilty. *(Lights down on Delbert, up on "courtroom;" sound of gavel.)*

ROBERT'S JUDGE. *(Thick Southern accent. Bangs gavel.)* Gentlemen, you have the right to remain silent. Anything you say can and will be used against you in a court of law. If you cannot afford an attorney, one will be appointed for you. Does everyone understand that? *(Beat.)*

You can answer that question. *(Small beat.)* Yes? *(Murmurs from seated group.)* Good.

Robert Hayes.

COURT ATTORNEY. He's in the first chair, Your Honor.

JUDGE. Mr. Hayes. *(No response, then beat.)* Mr. Hayes.

ROBERT. *(Very softly; head down.)* Yeah.

COURT ATTORNEY. Your Honor, he hears the court. He just doesn't want to show his face to the cameras, which is —

JUDGE. I want him to respond to me. Mr. —

ROBERT. *(Looking up.)* I *said* yes.

JUDGE. Okay. Mr. Hayes, you're charged with murder in the first degree. We find probable cause the accused committed the offense. He'll be held on no bond.

COURT ATTORNEY. Your Honor, Mr. Hayes has indicated that he does not wish to speak to anyone from law enforcement without an attorney present.

JUDGE. Okay, Mr. Hayes, can you afford a lawyer?

ROBERT. No.

JUDGE. Are you employed?

ROBERT. I *was*.

JUDGE. Do you own any property?

ROBERT. No.

JUDGE. Do you have any bank accounts?

ROBERT. No.

JUDGE. Do you have an automobile?

ROBERT. No.

JUDGE. The court will find that Mr. Hayes is indigent. Appoint the public defender to represent him. *(Sound of gavel.)*

COURT ATTORNEY. Thank you. *(Lights down on "courtroom," up on Delbert.)*

DELBERT. This is a weird country, man, it really is. It always amazes me when I talk about this. I say, "How do you figure this, now: All these guys, they been to Vanderbilt and to Yale and to Princeton and Harvard and shit, they look at the same information and they come up with diametrically opposite conclusions. Figure that out."

So it doesn't have anything to do with one's intelligence, it has to do with one's preconceptions, with one's *tendencies,* and how one looks at other human *beings* — you see, *that's* what it's about. *(Lights down on Delbert, up on Kerry, Kerry's Prosecutor, Kerry's Defense and Kerry's Judge.)*

KERRY. So they had a lead that the victim's boyfriend, Professor Whitfield, had done the murder. But they didn't go after him, they went after me. They said the crime was done by a homosexual maniacal murderer who hated women. The prosecution accused me of bein' a homosexual — before the jury —

PROSECUTION. *(Thick Texas accent.)* A young woman lies in her grave not far from this courtroom, butchered, because of Kerry Max Cook's warped homosexual lust for blood and perversion —

DEFENSE. Objection, Your Honor. The defendant's alleged homosexuality has nothing to do with the allegations in the murder indictment.

JUDGE. Objection will be overruled.

DEFENSE. We would then request an instruction to the Jury that they cannot consider —

JUDGE. — that motion is also overruled —

DEFENSE. We would then request the Court to declare a mistrial in this case —

JUDGE. — *Overruled.* Proceed, Counsel. *(Lights slowly go out on Kerry's Defense and Judge during the Prosecutor's speech. Lights remain up on Kerry and Prosecutor.)*

PROSECUTION. Thank you, Your Honor. *(To audience; with crescendoing fervor.)* Ladies and Gentlemen of the Jury. I would be remiss in my duty if I did not show you every last grotesque detail because the killer sits right before you in this courtroom and it is time for twelve good people from this county to put that man on the scrap heap of humanity where he belongs. He has a warped perversion and he will not reason with you. The victim was a young woman just beginning to realize her dreams and he butchered her body. This is the kind of sick perversion that turns Kerry Max Cook on.

You people have no right to even submit prison guards to the kind of risk that man poses. Think about it. Do you want to give this pervert his butcher knife back? Now, we must look upon it as putting a sick animal to sleep. Kerry Max Cook has forfeited his right to walk among us. He no longer has rights.

So let's let all the freaks and perverts and murderous homosexuals of the world know what we do with them in a court of justice. That we take their lives. *(Lights out on Kerry and Prosecution; up on Sunny.)*

SUNNY. My husband Jesse was tried first, and he had a past record, from when he was seventeen years old, and his trial lasted four days. We both had, of course, no good attorneys, no dream team, no expert witnesses, and so he was convicted, and sentenced to death.

My trial came later. I thought, surely that won't happen to *me*, I mean, I was a hippie, I'm one of those peace and love people, I'm a *vegetarian!* How could you possibly think I would kill someone?

And so I thought I'd go in, they'd figure out I didn't kill anyone, and they'd let it go. But that's not how it works. There was prosecutorial misconduct, there was hiding of evidence that would have proven I didn't do it; the jury wasn't even allowed to know that Rhodes accepted a plea bargain of three life sentences in exchange for his testimony! Now, I don't think three life sentences is a bargain. Nobody *I* know would think it's a bargain …

And I didn't have any investigators, I didn't have any expert witnesses, I didn't have thousands of dollars. My parents said, "Well, you know, we were told we could try and get you a better lawyer, but you *have* a lawyer, they've *appointed* you one, so it's okay." We didn't know. (*Lights down on Sunny; up on David, his Prosecution and Defense, sparring verbally.*)

DAVID'S PROSECUTION. The state respectfully submits to this jury that in that grocery store, David Keaton actually fired at Sheriff Carroll in order to come to the assistance of his co-defendant, who was in the process of cold-bloodedly murdering and killing Officer Khomas Revels. It's just as clear and simple as that. As a matter of fact, that is actually the truth.

DAVID'S DEFENSE. It was a quiet and peaceful Sunday night before David Keaton, then eighteen years old, was speedily whisked away to Quincy Jail. He was not told the reason for his arrest, nor was his family informed.

PROSECUTION. They're gonna tell you that all of Keaton's answers were suggested by the officers, that he was framed. Not by one officer, now; not by two officers, but by three or more State and County law enforcement officers.

DEFENSE. He was questioned without benefit of counsel, despite his request to his interrogators to call his mother and obtain legal assistance. At eleven P.M., Keaton was taken to the jail in Tallahassee, where questioning resumed and continued until the next morning.

PROSECUTION. Now, Keaton could have said in his statement anything he wanted to. There was nobody making those defendants say anything, and this jury knows anyway that of course that would be impossible, impractical. You just can't *make* somebody say something; nobody can!

DEFENSE. There is a law in this state that any person arrested shall be taken without delay and have the charges read in open court. The defendant was arrested on a Sunday. Well, this courthouse is open on Monday, and it's open on Tuesday, Wednesday, Thursday too. The defendant was not taken before a judge until Friday, although he had been arrested the Sunday before.

Now, I have nothing but respect for the Deputy Sheriffs, but I recognize, too, that it was a member of their staff that was killed. Wouldn't it be understandable for them to be more — *emotionally involved* in the investigation? (*Lights down on David, Prosecution and Defense; up on Sunny.*)

SUNNY. They tell you exactly how they're gonna do it. They're gonna send 2,200 volts of electricity through your body until you're dead. And then they ask you if you have anything to say to that, and really it's kind of dumbfounding. So after the judge read the sentence, I just said, "Are you finished?" I didn't have anything to say. What do you say? How can you say anything to that? *(Sound of cell door slamming shut. Lights up on Delbert, down on Sunny)*

DELBERT. I don't remember any of my dreams from when I was on death row. I almost never recall my dreams, which I am absolutely fascinated by.

When I was at the University of Chicago, I took part in a laboratory experiment. They were running a test to see if creative people's dreams differ from those who are less creative. And so of course, it appealed to the ego in me, thinking somebody thought I was creative.

So you go to bed in the lab and they are monitoring your respiration and your REM and so forth. And they would wake me up over the microphone and it always sounded to me like one of the Nazi doctors 'cause he had an accent, you know, he would be like, "MISTA TIBBS, YOU VERE DREAMINK." And I wanted to say, "No shit."

But the fascinating thing was, when the motherfuckers hooked me up — they put the receptors by your ears, right exactly at the same place they do when they're getting ready to execute your ass. *(Lights down on Delbert, up on Sunny.)*

SUNNY. Instead of sending me to be Jesse's cellmate, they decided to clear out an entire disciplinary unit at the women's prison. It's a very old prison, it's like a dungeon-type place. It was six steps from the door to the toilet bowl — you could stretch out your arms and touch both walls. They take your clothes, they give you a number, so basically they're taking — who you *are* from you. You no longer have a name, you're a number, you're locked inside this *tomb*. It's like you're thrown to the bottom of the well. *(Lights down on Sunny, up on David.)*

DAVID. There was one woman, lived across the street when I was a little boy, she had a goiter on her neck. And I was sayin', "Lord, if I only had the power of the Spirit, I would go lay my hands on her and her illness would disappear." And that's all I want, just to let the spirit be operatin' through me, whether it be knowledge, discernment, speak the word or whatever. *(To God.)* I would love to just do that before I die.

I had a relationship to God when I got in here, but somehow I've lost it. I guess I'm still reachin' out to find it — you know, I said some nights now I wanna light me a couple candles, lay back and just meditate, 'cause they say the kingdom of God is within you, isn't it? You know, everybody lookin' for something outward, but then, that light's *within* you, that voice we speak to … *(Whispering God's voice.)* "C'mon, boy."

Give you the chills when I say that, right? *(Lights down on David, up on Kerry.)*

KERRY. You know, when I was in there, I saw 141 guys go down. All's I got to do is pick up the newspaper, turn on the news, "such and such becomes the two-hundred-twenty-second inmate executed resulting from capital punishment," — and I hear the name and I say, "oh my God," 'cause I know him, I mean, I don't just *know* him, I *ate* with him, I *cried* with him, we used to play basketball and talk about, "man, you're gonna go free."

You know, I got a book, a book about Texas death row, and seriously, this book is what, five years old, and everyone in here has been executed. I can go through that book, one by one, and point out every face in here that's gone.

VOICEOVER/INMATE. Executed. *(Sound of switch being thrown.)* Executed. *(Sound of switch being thrown.)* Executed. *(Sound of switch being thrown.)*

KERRY. And you know, at a capital trial, the prosecutors always say, "He's dangerous, he's a maniac, the sick, twisted murderer." But I'm no different from you — I mean, I wasn't a street thug, I wasn't trash, I came from a good family — if it happened to me, man, it can happen to anyone. *(Lights down on Kerry, up on Gary.)*

GARY. I was in X-house — the execution house. That place was like somethin' out of a movie. There were no guards. They would just open your cell door and let you run around. I guess they figured, you were gonna die anyway, so why not.

So you can walk around through this dimly lit series of corridors, and through the observation room, into the execution room. That's where the phone was that all of us used. Which was also the phone that the governor would use to call in and stop an execution.

The whole place was run by gangs, you know, there was ongoing warfare between the different factions. And the only gang open to white guys was the Northsiders — which is basically made up of the Aryan Nation and the Skinheads. So I had no gang protection. So I kept to myself a lot. Killed a lot of time on my own.

One way I killed time, was I found a sewing needle stuck in a concrete wall. Somebody had smuggled it in. So I taught myself embroidery.

You'd take extra clothing — the blue jeans made real good blue thread. And I was lucky — I had kept my old yellow jumpsuit that they gave me to wear when I first went in. So that gave me yellow. You take your sheet apart, that gives you white. So I had three colors of thread, just from unraveling cloth. I made myself a tote bag I'd take to chow hall, and I embroidered flowers on it. I put bell-bottoms on a couple of my prison blues, made a Calvin and Hobbes patch I put on my hat. They confiscated that one. *(Lights down on Gary, up on Robert.)*

ROBERT. The electric chair was downstairs and I was upstairs, and every Wednesday morning they cranked that electric chair up and you could hear it buzz.

And when they served breakfast, you gotta have sharp ears to hear that front door open, 'cause if you oversleep, the roaches and the rats come and eat your breakfast, and that's the God's honest truth.

And the guards — I think nine times out of ten, the average person that became a guard, the only way I can see it, when he grew up he was a little runt and then the bigger guy would mess with him and all of that. And then they grow up and they wanna do that too.

When I was in there, one day, this officer was harassing my neighbor and I was a witness. And the other inmate, he wanted to write the officer up, he asked me —

BLACK INMATE. Hey Robert, would you sign this statement?

ROBERT. I said, I told him, yeah.

But a couple of days later, the officer came back to work, and something just told me to pay attention to him. *(Lights up on White Guard.)* And sure enough this officer, he read that statement, he gonna get back at me. He gonna spit off in my tea. And I *seen* him spit off in my tea. And so I said — *(To Guard.)* "Now why would you do that?"

WHITE GUARD. Do what? I didn't do that.

ROBERT. Hold on, I'm gonna prove it to you. *(To audience.)* And I went and got me a piece of toilet paper — *(Miming.)* — twisted it up, and put it directly on top of that tea. And I went 'round it. And I said — *(To Guard.)* "Now what is that? You can have my tea. You can take that shit back, MOTHERFUCKER." *(Lights down on Guard; lights shift on Robert. With increasing intensity:)* Robert E. Hayes, #95-19817, May 21, 1996.

Judge Kaplan,

I am writing to you in regards to some matters which I am having in this jail. The superintendent decline to answer any of my grievances so I am makin' you aware of this before I get charged this time for something I DID do. The problem is this Officer Santiago, who has constantly been provoking me. He come into my cell and toss my legal papers around, just tryin' to provoke me to fight him.

And today, he got classification to relocate me to the day room of a special wing for drug offenders. And by law they isn't supposed to have anyone sleeping in the day room no matter what wing it's in.

With my luck, some other inmate, some snitch, will get one of my legal briefs while I am sleeping, call the State, say Robert Hayes confessed to me so he can get himself a deal, and say "if you let me out I'll testify against him." And you, Judge Kaplan, will believe that fuck shit.

So Judge, I am askin' you to grant me an order stating that me and the stated officer be kept away from one another, because I am *not* goin' to take *any more* of his *bull shit! (Small beat.)* But thank you for your time. I'm sure I'll see you on another charge if you refuse to keep Santiago away from me.

Robert Hayes. *(Light up on Georgia.)*

GEORGIA. And, okay, some snitch *did* get a hold of one of his legal briefs. Just like Robert said. *(Lights down on Robert and Georgia; up on Kerry.)*

KERRY. So, uh, they accused me of bein' a homosexual, and that got into the media that got to death row even before I got there, so in prison, uh, uh — I was uh, uh — *(Pause.)* — I had three guys pull a train on me ... and they raped me, and sodomized me, and they carved "good p-u-s-s-y" on my behind. And it's there all over my body, its cut so deep I can't, plastic surgery won't remove it, it's not a tattoo, and I attempted suicide a couple times with this whole little war I was fighting: On the one side, the criminal justice system, and then on the Western front I'm fighting with fear of my life with these inmates every day. *(Lights up on Delbert.)*

DELBERT. Needless to say, Job is one of my favorite Biblical figures. *(Lights down on Kerry.)* I don't know if I have the patience of Job — but I hope I have his faith. Even if you got a teeny weeny bit it's big. The shit is hard to come by, you know what I'm sayin'?

But faith or not, I realized a long time ago, if I internalized all the anger, and all the pain, and all the hurt, I'd be dead already — they wouldn't even have to execute me. *(Lights down on Delbert, up on David.)*

DAVID. When I was inside, one time, I felt this feelin' came over me where I felt the longin' of God for his people, I felt his love for his people, his desire for his people not to be cast aside. You know,

I felt all this, and here I was on death row. It was so heavy. God, it was a burden on me.

And I was feelin' all this, and we went outside for recreation, and in the yard out there you have a little basketball court, shuffleboard court, and there's a curtain up with the electric chair showin'. You look right up there, you can see the chair. You know, even if you playin', they gotta remind you that you still gonna die, 'cause here's the chair. *(Sound of thunderclap and rain.)* But then it starts stormin' man —

I looked up, raise my hand and I said "In the name of Jesus, I command this rain to stop." *(Sound of "swoosh" and rain stops.)* This guy says, "Man, you do it one more time, I'm gonna become a believer!" So it started again — *(Sound of thunder and rain.)* So I said it again. "In the name of Jesus, I command this rain to stop." *(Sound of "swoosh" and rain stops.)* It stopped. He said, "Man, you do it *one more time* — "

So it started back … same thing. *(Sound of thunder and rain.)* "In the name of Jesus, I command this rain to stop." *(Sound of "swoosh" and rain stops.)* But this time he didn't say nothin'. He just looked at me like "Hmmm," you know.

But it didn't rain anymore, until we finished playin', and we had to go back inside. And when the last man stepped through the door, the whole world just burst open. *(Sound of thunder and rain.)* It rained for the rest of the night. *(Lights down on David, up on Sunny. Rain fades slowly over the beginning of Sunny's speech.)*

SUNNY. I have fifteen years' worth of letters between me and Jesse. I saved not only the letters, but the envelopes, because anything that he touched, or that he wrote on, or that he licked with his tongue, I was keeping. I didn't even read his letters when I first got them; I would carry 'em around with me for a while. Just to hold it. I'd see if he put the stamp on right side up or upside down. That was part of his message too.

And then I'd open it and I wouldn't read it for content; I would just look at it to see: Did he look like he was happy when he wrote it, or sad? Did the writing slant upward or downward? Oh it's big round open letters; he must have been having a good day. Oh it's very tight writing, I can see he must have been having some problems. I would just savor the whole thing, and *then* I'd read it.

We carried on a fairly full life in our letters, actually, including our sex life. Oh yeah. *(Laughter.)* You know, you have to send your letters out unsealed so that they can read them to see that there's no escape plans or whatever. So we got ourselves little Japanese dictionaries, and we used the Japanese language for our lovemaking, because we wanted to have some privacy. *(Lights up on Jesse.)*

JESSE. September 30th, 1976.

My Dearest Sunny,

I love you. It's about eleven P.M. now. I'm sitting here on my bunk. The TV is on with the sound off and on the channel that is just fuzzy so that I can use it for light. I'm reading *King Lear* and *Hamlet*, if you can believe that. I've been studying too much law lately and need to give my head something relaxing too. I received your beautiful letter and … two pictures of the kids. We're so lucky. I love you so much. You're my woman, as close as my breath. You're the strongest female I've ever known. Hand and glove, you know?

Never be lonesome, we're only separated by miles. This won't last either, believe that. I sure would like to speak to you alone, let's say for a few hours —

Hito banju kimyo ikasatai.

Kimito ito tsuni naritai.

My place or yours. And don't worry, I'm on the case, lover.

I love you, Mama.

Jesse *(Lights down on Jesse.)*

SUNNY. And so we had this life, you know; this little world together. I existed on those letters. *(Lights down on Sunny, up on Kerry.)*

KERRY. I was holding on for my brother — I can't tell you how close we were, he wasn't just a big brother, I *worshiped* him, he was my *role model*, he was everything I wasn't — he didn't smoke pot, he made straight A's in school — and I was the black sheep of the family. My brother was always trying to rescue me, very strict on me — *(Lights up on Doyle.)*

DOYLE. No, Kerry, I'm gonna *lose* you, I'm gonna *lose* you, you're gonna get hurt —

KERRY. — and then there I was, sitting on death row.

He was taking up for me my whole life. I was just always a real soft sensitive person, you know, and I guess I had so many girlfriends 'cause I was so sensitive, I don't mean girlfriends like girls *sexually*, I mean friends that are girls.

And so my brother — the last time I touched him was at the Smith County jail — he reached in and held my hand and was crying and said —

DOYLE. It's not over, Kerry, 'cause you're not gonna die, you're gonna get out.

KERRY. I was the baby of the family and my brother would come visit me and I would have these black eyes and stuff, you know, and he said —

DOYLE. I want you to tell me who did this to you, I'm going to talk to the warden.

KERRY. *(To Doyle.)* "You don't understand, you'll get me killed, that's called snitching, that's the worst thing you can do." *(To audience.)* So I forced my brother — when he thought he could help me, I took that away from him too, saying "you can't help me, I'm on my own now." And so, uh — *(Pause.)* — he started drinking.

The guy had it all, man, he was a senior supervisor at this huge corporation company, and he fell into a bottle, lost his wife, lost his kids, he'd sit around in a dark room and get drunk and talk about his little brother, why isn't he coming home. He put himself right on death row with me.

And he's workin' as an assistant manager at a McDonald's in downtown Jacksonville, and there's this guy named Jeff works there. Jeff said that my brother liked him because my brother told him — You're a lot like my little brother Kerry — and that's how they got to be friends.

So anyway, one night after work they go to this club in Tyler, Texas, and they're shooting pool. You know how you get when you're drinking beer and you're hot with the stick.

And right now it's closing and my brother's running the table on this one last guy — and he says to Jeff —

DOYLE. You go, I'll be out there in a minute.

KERRY. And Jeff's walking out of the club, and there were these two black guys sitting on the table, and one of them's wearing sunglasses, and Jeff reaches up — he's just playing — takes the glasses and puts them on — *(Jeff mimics Stevie Wonder.)* and mimics Stevie Wonder. And the guy says —

BLACK GUY 2. Say, what's up on you, man?

KERRY. — and this guy jumps off the table and gets real aggressive, and he's like —

BLACK GUY 2. I'm gonna bring a world of hurt to him.

KERRY. And so about this time my brother walks up and says —

DOYLE. Hey, hey, man —

KERRY. My brother's really laid-back, you know, he wasn't a violent dude — I mean, he was a real laid-back, compassionate person. But Jeff just says —

JEFF. Man, fuck these people.

KERRY. And walks out. So my brother follows him outside. *(Beat. Lights shift.)* It's December 27th, 1997, it's really cold that night, and my brother and Jeff are both trying to get in the car but the locks are frozen, and this pickup truck pulls up behind my brother, and Jeff says —

JEFF. Hey — watch out!

KERRY. My brother turns around and this guy, he got out of the truck with his hand behind his back and he says —

BLACK GUY 2. Whatcha gonna do for me, white boy, you gonna call me nigger? Whatcha gonna do for me?

KERRY. There was all kinds of people standing around, and my brother told him —

DOYLE. Hey look man, we've all been drinking tonight — this is nothin' to have no misunderstanding about. Tomorrow morning you're gonna wake up and laugh about this.

KERRY. And he says —

BLACK GUY 2. Fuck you, man.

KERRY. — and he brings from around his back a big ole forty-four magnum and he shoots him — *(Loud, long gunshot.)* — and uh, uh, my brother — so weird man — he rose up and stood up, and Jeff walked over to him and he couldn't even tell he was shot, his eyes were fixated looking straight ahead. And Jeff said —

JEFF. Man, you okay? Man, you okay?

KERRY. — and blood started pouring out of my brother's nose and he fell . . . and he died on that parking lot.

And uh … *(Pause.)* with me being on death row, the D.A. was reluctant to take it to trial — she said the defense would claim that my brother had bragged that he had a brother on death row and he was bad.

And so they got my mom and dad to agree to a plea bargain, and the guy who killed my brother got ten years. And he got out in three.

My mother would look me in the eye and tell me that I'm responsible for my brother's murder. That if it weren't for me going to death row, he'd still be here. She would tell me that. I know it's going to sound corny there, but — and I mean it — every day that goes by I wished I could tell him how much I love him. So while you've got it man, never take it for granted, 'cause you never know. *(Lights down on Kerry, up on Sunny.)*

SUNNY. First I had to decide: "This is bullshit, I am not going to let them do this to me." 'Cause if you sit there, rubbing two sticks together and crying on your sticks, they're never gonna make a spark. But, you know, if you stop feeling sorry for yourself, just because you're determined not to believe in hopelessness, then a spark happens, and then you just keep fanning that little spark until you got a flame.

And I realized that it was like a big trick. That I wasn't just a little lump of flesh that they could put in a cage. And I decided that I would have faith, that there was some power out there greater than them, to which I could make my appeal.

Now, you people that don't believe, you could say I was like Dumbo and I put this feather in my nose and I flew because I could fly anyway.

Or you could say that there is really something out there and that if we have faith in it and we appeal to it, it will answer us — and maybe we're both right. I don't know. *(Lights down on Sunny, up on Robert.)*

ROBERT. Well, see, before I went to prison, I had a dream about prison — and I seen death row, I seen the inside, and I seen myself get out. And 'cause a that dream, I always said, I'm gonna get a new trial. And sure enough, one day, I get awakened by all this commotion. All the inmates, they get up in the vents, hollerin' — *(Lights up on Men.)*

ALL MEN. *(Ad lib.)* Man, you got a new trial! Damn, Robert, you gonna go free! You on the radio! Turn on the radio! *(Etc.)*

CELLMATE. Put the radio on!

ROBERT. Well, I put the radio on.

And later that day, my lawyer came, and she said to me —

FEMALE LAWYER. Now, you know, Robert, if you lose, you can go back to death row.

ROBERT. And I said — *(To Lawyer.)* "Well, now, accordin' to that dream, I'm gonna go free."

And she said —

FEMALE LAWYER. *(To Robert.)* You gonna put all your trust in a dream?

ROBERT. And I said, "yep." *(Small beat. Lights up on Prosecution, Georgia and Ex-Boyfriend.)*

My lawyer had found a record that said that in the girl's hand when she died was some white people hair, red hair, sixteen inches long. So they said —

ROBERT'S PROSECUTION. When you were strangling this

girl, she reached up and pulled her own hair!

ROBERT. *(To Prosecution:)* Hold on. *(To audience:)* Now when someone come up behind you and they strangle you, are you gonna pull your own hair? Or are you gonna pull the hair of whoever back there behind you?

GEORGIA. Okay?!

ROBERT. *(To Prosecution:)* You can have a seat. *(Prosecution sits down. To audience:)* And we all knew this white guy, her ex-boyfriend. He had been asking the girl for a date, telling her —

EX-BOYFRIEND. Why you keep hanging out with all them blacks?

ROBERT. And he asked her that *same night* —

EX-BOYFRIEND. We gonna go out?

ROBERT. And she said, "We ain't."

And so my lawyer, she found out the cops had that hair, she found the guy. He got up and testified at my appeal.

So my lawyer ask him —

FEMALE LAWYER. Back in 1990, what color was your hair, and how long was it?

ROBERT. And by then he had short hair, salt and pepper, you know, and he said —

EX-BOYFRIEND. *(On the stand.)* My hair was the same color and length back then as it is now

ROBERT. And my lawyer said —

FEMALE LAWYER. Are you sure?

EX-BOYFRIEND. Of course I'm sure.

ROBERT. So my lawyer pulls out this envelope. And she said —

FEMALE LAWYER. Again in 1990, do you remember having your picture taken near the racetrack?

EX-BOYFRIEND. Uh, yeah.

ROBERT. And then she pulled that big ol' photograph picture out and showed it to him. And there he was, his hair red and brown and sixteen inches long on the picture. *(Robert looks to Georgia.)*

ROBERT and GEORGIA. Okay?! *(Lights down on Robert, Georgia, Ex-Boyfriend and Lawyer; up on Kerry.)*

KERRY. So then after I've been on death row for twenty-two years, they find this DNA evidence, you know, and the prosecution says that this will be the final nail in Kerry Max Cook's coffin: "We'll show the world once and for all that he committed that murder." And then the results come in and it did just the opposite, it finally took the nail out of my coffin, told the world the truth — that that was Professor Whitfield's DNA they found on that girl.

And he's still out. They never even went after him. He's been walking around a free man, laughing at the system for twenty-two years. Twenty-two years. *(Lights down on Kerry, up on Gary.)*

GARY. About halfway through my time on death row, a lawyer named Larry Marshall took on my case. He's at Northwestern, he works with a bunch of law students on wrongful convictions. My twin sister found out about him and went down there literally through a blinding snowstorm to see if he would take me on. And he said yes.

Man, that was like the cavalry coming.

Once he started working on it, Larry found out about this motorcycle gang called the Outlaws. Guys gained entrance into the gang by performing violent acts: They killed a bunch of people, they'd bomb the Hell's Angels — they'd just do a lot of stuff. And the federal government, the ATF, was running wiretaps on them. Well, in 1995, the ATF got a videotaped confession from an Outlaw guy saying he killed my parents. But I wasn't released until 1996. And that whole year in between, they were fighting my appeal. They fought it all the way to the Illinois Supreme Court.

The two guys who killed my parents were just found guilty last year.

But I've been adamant that those guys not get the death penalty. Some people think that's stupid, but why would I want them to die? It's not gonna bring my parents back. No good's gonna come from it. *(Lights down on Gary; up on Sunny and Rhodes.)*

SUNNY. *(To audience.)* In 1979, Walter Rhodes wrote the following letter to a judge.

RHODES. I, Walter Norman Rhodes, hereby depose and say that I am under no duress nor coercion to execute this affidavit. This statement is made freely and voluntarily, and to purge myself before my Creator.

Briefly. On February 20th, 1976, at approximately seven-fifteen A.M., I did, in fact, shoot to death two law enforcement officers with a nine millimeter Browning pistol.

I state emphatically and unequivocally that my previous testimony against Jesse Tafero and Sonia Jacobs was *false* and part of the statements I was instructed to make by the assistant state attorney, who did coerce me into lying.

I took a polygraph examination relative to this case, but owing to the fact that I am a student of Yoga and Karaté, and have been for the last ten years, I passed it. And can pass any such test, in my opinion.

The foregoing statements are true and correct to the best of my knowledge and belief. I so swear.

Walter Norman Rhodes, Jr., 9 November 1979. *(Lights down on Rhodes.)*

SUNNY. Keep in mind that I wasn't released until 1992.

So I'll just give you a moment to reflect: From 1976 to 1992, just remove that entire chunk from your life, and that's what happened. *(Long pause, the length of a six-count.)*

But after all that, one day, the guard came into my cell and told me I was getting out. I thought he was trying to trick me. *(Sound of cell door opening; Sunny takes it in.)* And it was just so *joyous.* I mean, I know a lot of people are angry, and I was angry some, but I didn't want to waste my time being mad.

At first I did everything that Jesse and I said we were going to do together. I went to New York City, I went to the bookstore we said we were going to go to, I bought the book we said we were going to buy to make our Japanese gardens. I was doing it all for both of us. *(Lights down on Sunny; up on Delbert.)*

DELBERT. When I first got out, I was numb. I didn't sleep for the first three days. I couldn't. And on death row, I had slept like a baby every night.

My first day home, they threw a party at my brother's house. My brother. He gave me his bed for the night, you know with a red velvet coverlet on it and everything. And one of the sisters from the Defense Committee — she spent the night with me — which was nice, you know.

But I just couldn't get the fuck to sleep, man, and I guess around the third night I began hallucinating, and one of my friends said, let me call my Pastor and ask him to pray for you. And I talked to the Pastor, and he said some kind of prayer and I laid down and went straight to sleep. I haven't had any problems sleeping since then.

After that, the main adjustment was just learning to feel again. You know, when you're in prison, you can't allow yourself to feel too much. So when you get out, you've gotta practice. I had to practice a bunch to be human again. To remind me. *(Lights down on Delbert, up on David.)*

DAVID. Maybe I'm still in there, in a way. 'Cause after I was out, I would go to work, I would come home, I would shut the door, and I would lock it. Just like in prison. Go to work, go to the store, come home, lock the door, click. Then one day I saw. "What're you doing, lockin' the door?" I say. "Don't you know you're free now? You're not in lock-up anymore, man — you're free!"

Prison took away that — spark for life, okay, 'cause in my old pictures from high school, I can see in my face — I'm smilin', you know. And now that's somethin' people round here don't see me do too much, smile. *(Sound of rain. David looks up, acknowledges the rain. Halfheartedly:)* In the name of J — *(Rain does not stop. Another half-try:)* In the name of Jesus — *(Rain does not stop. David gives up trying. Rain continues softly under the following and slowly fades.)* Prison really did somethin' to me.

And now, I do a lot of things — like I may drink, okay, and I smoke some marijuana — to cocaine, to crack cocaine. A perfect day, to me, would be, just to get plastered, you know, to forget. 'Cause now I'm tryin to find out who I am, and if I smoke a joint of reefer, it takes me to that point where I can sit down and write me some poetry or whatever, just like I useta do.

But what are you gonna do? I mean, if they're in power and you have no power, then you're through. Bein' little is like bein' up next to a large oak tree and you just a little small pine. *(Beat.)*

That's why, like I said, I really gotta get back into a spirituality thing and focus on findin' that light within ... 'cause that's all I really got, you know. *(Lights down on David; up on Kerry and Sandra.)*
SANDRA. Actually I am not a bleeding heart liberal at all, as a matter of fact I had a family member murdered and I was always a believer in the death penalty —
KERRY. She's a scientist —
SANDRA. But I was on the board of directors at the Dallas Peace Center and a guy from Amnesty approached me one day and told me he wanted me to help Kerry get integrated into society.

So we were supposed to meet at this conference, and this *boy* walks in, I mean, he had on some jeans and any piece of clothing that had a zipper — you know, from the seventies — it had to have a zipper or he didn't want it, he had grown his hair out and he dyed it — because, you know, he's really nineteen at heart ... he couldn't look at anyone, he looked down, his leg was shaking the whole time.
KERRY. Especially with a female, man, I was super traumatized about that. Very shy.
SANDRA. He got up and used the bathroom probably about twenty times because he was so nervous —
KERRY. Aw, man, don't tell 'em that —

SANDRA. But then I thought — and I'm ashamed to have had this thought — what did he do to get himself in that situation? That's how I looked at it ... 'cause you know, I was very conservative — *(Beat.)* and also very stupid. But he gave me the evidence, the hardcore evidence, and it dawned on me, oh my God, how could this have happened?

KERRY. The state of Texas executed me over a thousand times, man, and it just keeps on doin' it. I get nightmares — sometimes I forget I'm really here. And every day when I get in the shower I'm reminded of it, 'cause I cannot avoid the scars all over my body. This is the only woman I've been with since I've been free, 'cause of that, and I married her. Think I'm gonna keep her.

But I'll be honest with you: The price of being here, alive, in this room, is really extraordinary — because when I'm alone, man, especially at night — *(Beat.)* Talk about a mental trip, huh? *(Lights down on Kerry and Sandra, up on Robert and Georgia.)*

ROBERT. I been out now, three and a half years goin' on four. And we got married, what?

GEORGIA. *(Proud.)* Two years, 'bout two years —

ROBERT. And she be wanting me to come home, you know at night, and I don't want to come home, I wanna stay out, you know, 'cause if I come home — *(Joking.)* — it makes me feel like I *still locked up.* *(Georgia responds.)* And you know, there's a lotta times when she go to the store, and she had to knock on the door to let me know she coming in.

GEORGIA. Yeah, he jumps! When I first moved in, I just be walking in, walking out, and he just jump up, 'cause he's just in that mode! I'm like, okay, he has to take a minute to calm down 'cause he's just used to that. You know, stuff like that plays with your mind.

ROBERT. Yeah, I was in there seven and a half years and it ain't ever gonna go away, far as I'm concerned. Lost my relaxation. Lotta other things too. You know, you can't really put your thoughts on what you could have lost, or what you *have* lost. I said I could have been a millionaire, or I could have been the Police Chief. I could have been one of the famous black horse trainers —

GEORGIA. And they won't even give him his license back.

ROBERT. The Trotting Association, they wouldn't even give me my racing license back.

GEORGIA. Can you believe that?

ROBERT. I went to the County, I passed my test with flying colors. They asked me have I ever been convicted of a crime. I put down on the application no, because the Supreme Court, they overturned it. Well, they wrote me back and told me I lied.

GEORGIA. Tell 'em what you told your cousin.

ROBERT. So I told my cousin, I said, well watch. I can go to a gun shop around here, I'm gonna see if they're gonna deny me. I went and got the gun. But the racing commission wouldn't give me my license back. I can legally get a gun, but I can't get a license to drive a horse.

GEORGIA. He can't do something he *likes* to do.

ROBERT. Can't do something I like to do.

And you know, all I want is, I would like to have me this woman here, a nice piece of land in the country, a nice barn, tractor and a couple of horses. I don't ask for much. But they sayin' I can't. *(Small beat.)* Because of their mistake. *(Lights down on Robert and Georgia, up on Gary and Sue.)*

GARY. What's the matter?

SUE. *(To Gary.)* I had an incident at the market today, and, and I don't know why it upset me so much, but it really upset me. Some — well —

Well, it was awful. It was — it was about you.

GARY. What, at the market? Somebody didn't like the produce?

SUE. No … *(To audience.)* I mean, this has been over three years now, and this guy was like, you know — *(To Gary.)* It started out he just wanted to buy beets. Said — *(Lights up on Farmer.)*

FARMER. I want a bushel of beets.

SUE. And I told him — *(To Farmer.)* "Well, all of our produce is certified organic." And he says —

FARMER. Oh, you grew all of this just in water?

SUE. I'm like — *(To Farmer.)* "no, that's hydroponic." And he asks me —

FARMER. Where do you farm?

SUE. And I told him. So he said —

FARMER. *Oh,* so you farm with that guy that was in all that trouble.

SUE. Oh, you mean Gary? Yeah, he's my husband.

FARMER. Yeah, that was sort of a fishy case, wasn't it?

SUE. Well, you know, two bikers just confessed and were convicted.

FARMER. Well, Gauger confessed too. You know, the paper *said.* *(Lights down on Farmer.)*

GARY. *(To Sue.)* There's gonna be idiots. I mean, that guy, you know, he's living a lie, just like the newspapers or the prosecutors or whatever. Everyone perceives things in their own way, so which one is the reality, you know? Is the reality your perception? Or is it a composite of everybody's perception, or what? *(To audience.)* I mean, what is reality? We're all light beams, you know.

SUE. Oh, no, Gary, don't go there —

GARY. We're all light beams. People wonder, how could God create miracles? Well, because God moves at the speed of light, and time stops, you see. Once you get to the speed of light, you got all the time in the world to change things and create miracles.

SUE. *(Bemused.)* Oh, so you're an expert now?

GARY. It's all there on a molecular level, you know. Once somebody told me God is DNA, and you look how tenacious that stuff is you start to wonder. *(Lights down on Gary and Sue, up on Sunny.)*

SUNNY. You see, I got another chance, because I looked for it. I looked to turn a pile of manure into flowers. I didn't even get lemons, I got manure. *(Laughs.)*

I mean, I'm not glad for what happened to me — when I was in there my parents died, my children grew up without a family … and my husband was executed — very, very brutally. Jesse's execution was known worldwide. The chair malfunctioned and made a mess of it. And — *(Pause.)* they had to pull the switch three times.

And he didn't die. It took *thirteen and a half* minutes for Jesse to die. Three jolts of electricity that lasted fifty-five seconds each. Almost a minute. *Each.* Until finally flames shot out from his head, and smoke came from his ears, and the people that came to see the execution, on behalf of the press, are still writing about it. *Ten years afterwards.*

Why do we do that? *(Lights down on Sunny, up on Delbert.)*

DELBERT. Mahatma Gandhi said that once he discovered who God was, all fears left him regarding the rest of the world, you know, and it's *true*, you know. If you're not harboring any kind of malice, any kind of stuff like that in your heart, there really ain't too much to be afraid of.

And I understand why people are afraid, I mean, I do think the world itself, if you think about it, can be quite frightening — *(Pause.)* I mean just like getting up every day, you know, I understand.

But you can't give in to that. 'Cause as they say in the cowboy pictures, nobody's gonna live forever, you know what I'm sayin'? And if you have to go, then you might as well go being about the highest thing that you can be about. And that means learning not to fear other people, man, on a *human* level, white or black or *whatever.*

I mean, it's a real struggle not to lump all white people — you

51

know, if you're locked up in a room and a guy comes in wearin' a gray suit and he hits you every time he walks into the room, afterwards you gonna have a thing about people with gray suits, I don't give a fuck who they are.

But I try not to look at the world monolithically like that, and that's what has helped me to survive. I mean, I think the American criminal justice system is totally fucked up — I think some things about our *country* are fucked up — but I also think it's a great country, you know, I really do.

But I mean, the fact that you can have people who probably knew that a lotta folks were innocent — but *they* were not gonna be the ones to lose their jobs, jeopardize their kids' college education, blow their new S.U.V. or whatever, for some abstraction like justice. *(Beat.)* That's fucked up.

And I know America gets tired of all of these people talking about what they don't have and what's wrong with the country. Folks say "well what's right with the country?" Well, what the fuck? To make things *better*, we ain't interested in what's *right* with it, we're interested in what's *wrong* with it. You don't say "what's *right* with my car?" What's *wrong* with it is what we better deal with. *(Lights up on Sunny.)*

SUNNY. I want to be a living memorial. When I die I want 'em to plant tomatoes on me, or apple trees or something, so that I can still be part of things. And while I'm still alive, I'm planting my seeds everywhere I go, so that they'll say, "I once heard this woman, and she didn't let them stop her, and she didn't get crushed, and if that little woman person can do it, then I can do it." And *that's* my revenge. That's my legacy, and my memorial.

You know, I've never been to Jesse's grave, and for a long time it was a bone of contention between his mother and me. But I explained to her, I said that grave is not where Jesse really is. I said, that grave is your monument, and this is mine. My life is my monument.

DELBERT.
This
is the place for thoughts that do not end in concreteness.
It is necessary to be curious
and dangerous to dwell here, to wonder why
and how and when is dangerous —
but *that's* how we get out of this hole.
It is not easy to be a poet here.
Yet I sing.

We sing.
(Sound of rain slowly fades in. To David, who does not see him. Lights glow on David.) Sing. *(David raises his hand to stop the rain. It does. He smiles to himself as Delbert watches. Blackout.)*

End of Play

SOUND EFFECTS

Banging of gavel
Gunshots
Cars honking, helicopters
Heavy gunfire
Crash, sirens
Cell door slamming shut
Switch being thrown
Thunderclap and rain
Swooshing sound as rain stops
Cell door opening
Sound of rain

NEW PLAYS

★ **AT HOME AT THE ZOO by Edward Albee.** Edward Albee delves deeper into his play THE ZOO STORY by adding a first act, HOMELIFE, which precedes Peter's fateful meeting with Jerry on a park bench in Central Park. "An essential and heartening experience." *–NY Times.* "Darkly comic and thrilling." *–Time Out.* "Genuinely fascinating." *–Journal News.* [2M, 1W] ISBN: 978-0-8222-2317-7

★ **PASSING STRANGE book and lyrics by Stew, music by Stew and Heidi Rodewald, created in collaboration with Annie Dorsen.** A daring musical about a young bohemian that takes you from black middle-class America to Amsterdam, Berlin and beyond on a journey towards personal and artistic authenticity. "Fresh, exuberant, bracingly inventive, bitingly funny, and full of heart." *–NY Times.* "The freshest musical in town!" *–Wall Street Journal.* "Excellent songs and a vulnerable heart." *–Variety.* [4M, 3W] ISBN: 978-0-8222-2400-6

★ **REASONS TO BE PRETTY by Neil LaBute.** Greg really, truly adores his girlfriend, Steph. Unfortunately, he also thinks she has a few physical imperfections, and when he mentions them, all hell breaks loose. "Tight, tense and emotionally true." *–Time Magazine.* "Lively and compulsively watchable." *–The Record.* [2M, 2W] ISBN: 978-0-8222-2394-8

★ **OPUS by Michael Hollinger.** With only a few days to rehearse a grueling Beethoven masterpiece, a world-class string quartet struggles to prepare their highest-profile performance ever—a televised ceremony at the White House. "Intimate, intense and profoundly moving." *–Time Out.* "Worthy of scores of bravissimos." *–BroadwayWorld.com.* [4M, 1W] ISBN: 978-0-8222-2363-4

★ **BECKY SHAW by Gina Gionfriddo.** When an evening calculated to bring happiness takes a dark turn, crisis and comedy ensue in this wickedly funny play that asks what we owe the people we love and the strangers who land on our doorstep. "As engrossing as it is ferociously funny." *–NY Times.* "Gionfriddo is some kind of genius." *–Variety.* [2M, 3W] ISBN: 978-0-8222-2402-0

★ **KICKING A DEAD HORSE by Sam Shepard.** Hobart Struther's horse has just dropped dead. In an eighty-minute monologue, he discusses what path brought him here in the first place, the fate of his marriage, his career, politics and eventually the nature of the universe. "Deeply instinctual and intuitive." *–NY Times.* "The brilliance is in the infinite reverberations Shepard extracts from his simple metaphor." *–TheaterMania.* [1M, 1W] ISBN: 978-0-8222-2336-8

DRAMATISTS PLAY SERVICE, INC.
440 Park Avenue South, New York, NY 10016 212-683-8960 Fax 212-213-1539
postmaster@dramatists.com www.dramatists.com

NEW PLAYS

★ **AUGUST: OSAGE COUNTY by Tracy Letts.** WINNER OF THE 2008 PULITZER PRIZE AND TONY AWARD. When the large Weston family reunites after Dad disappears, their Oklahoma homestead explodes in a maelstrom of repressed truths and unsettling secrets. "Fiercely funny and bitingly sad." –*NY Times.* "Ferociously entertaining." –*Variety.* "A hugely ambitious, highly combustible saga." –*NY Daily News.* [6M, 7W] ISBN: 978-0-8222-2300-9

★ **RUINED by Lynn Nottage.** WINNER OF THE 2009 PULITZER PRIZE. Set in a small mining town in Democratic Republic of Congo, RUINED is a haunting, probing work about the resilience of the human spirit during times of war. "A full-immersion drama of shocking complexity and moral ambiguity." –*Variety.* "Sincere, passionate, courageous." –*Chicago Tribune.* [8M, 4W] ISBN: 978-0-8222-2390-0

★ **GOD OF CARNAGE by Yasmina Reza, translated by Christopher Hampton.** WINNER OF THE 2009 TONY AWARD. A playground altercation between boys brings together their Brooklyn parents, leaving the couples in tatters as the rum flows and tensions explode. "Satisfyingly primitive entertainment." –*NY Times.* "Elegant, acerbic, entertainingly fueled on pure bile." –*Variety.* [2M, 2W] ISBN: 978-0-8222-2399-3

★ **THE SEAFARER by Conor McPherson.** Sharky has returned to Dublin to look after his irascible, aging brother. Old drinking buddies Ivan and Nicky are holed up at the house too, hoping to play some cards. But with the arrival of a stranger from the distant past, the stakes are raised even higher. "Dark and enthralling Christmas fable." –*NY Times.* "A timeless classic." –*Hollywood Reporter.* [5M] ISBN: 978-0-8222-2284-2

★ **THE NEW CENTURY by Paul Rudnick.** When the playwright is Paul Rudnick, expectations are geared for a play both hilarious and smart, and this provocative and outrageous comedy is no exception. "The one-liners fly like rockets." –*NY Times.* "The funniest playwright around." –*Journal News.* [2M, 3W] ISBN: 978-0-8222-2315-3

★ **SHIPWRECKED! AN ENTERTAINMENT—THE AMAZING ADVENTURES OF LOUIS DE ROUGEMONT (AS TOLD BY HIMSELF) by Donald Margulies.** The amazing story of bravery, survival and celebrity that left nineteenth-century England spellbound. Dare to be whisked away. "A deft, literate narrative." –*LA Times.* "Springs to life like a theatrical pop-up book." –*NY Times.* [2M, 1W] ISBN: 978-0-8222-2341-2

DRAMATISTS PLAY SERVICE, INC.
440 Park Avenue South, New York, NY 10016 212-683-8960 Fax 212-213-1539
postmaster@dramatists.com www.dramatists.com